Clothes

Around the World

Clare Lewis

Heinemann
LIBRARY

Chicago, Illinois

Edited by Joanna Issa, Shelly Lyons, Diyan Leake, and
Helen Cox Cannons
Designed by Cynthia Akiyoshi
Original illustrations © Capstone Global Library Ltd 2014
Picture research by Elizabeth Alexander and Tracy Cummins
Production by Victoria Fitzgerald
Originated by Capstone Global Library Ltd
Printed in the United States of America

042717 010482RP

Library of Congress Cataloging-in-Publication Data
Lewis, Clare.
   Clothes around the world / Clare Lewis.
       pages cm.—(Around the World.)
   Includes bibliographical references and index.
   ISBN 978-1-4846-0374-1 (hb)—ISBN 978-1-4846-0381-9
(pb) 1. Clothing and dress. I. Title.

GT511.L49 2015
391—dc23   2013040509

Acknowledgments
We would like to thank the following for permission to
reproduce photographs: Alamy pp. 8 & 22a (both © Horizons
WWP), 12 & 22d (both © Hemis), 16 (© Ian Shaw), 23b
(© Hemis), 23c (© Ian Shaw); Corbis pp. 17 & 23a (both
© Ocean), 21 (© Sean De Burca); Getty Images pp. 4
(Adam Hester), 11 (Ariel Skelley), 13 & 22b (both LEON
NEAL/AFP); Shutterstock pp. 1 (© 41), 2 (© Worldpics),
3 (© watin), 6 & 22c (both © Sofarina79), 7 (© Zoran
Karapancev), 10 (© tankist276), 14 (© Tatiana Morozova),
15 & 22c (both © df028), 24 (© Worldpics); Superstock pp.
5 (allindiaimages), 9 (age footstock), 18 (Juice Images), 19
(Stefan Kiefer/imageb /imagebroker.net), 20 (Design Pics).

Front cover photograph of a young girl performing in a
folk dance show in the Zocalo in Oaxaca City, Mexico,
reproduced with permission of Getty Images (Politzer/Lonely
Planet Images). Back cover photograph reproduced with
permission of Shutterstock (© Zoran Karapancev).

Every effort has been made to contact copyright holders
of material reproduced in this book. Any omissions will
be rectified in subsequent printings if notice is given to
the publisher.

All the Internet addresses (URLs) given in this book were
valid at the time of going to press. However, due to the
dynamic nature of the Internet, some addresses may have
changed, or sites may have changed or ceased to exist
since publication. While the author and publisher regret any
inconvenience this may cause readers, no responsibility for
any such changes can be accepted by either the author or
the publisher.

Contents

Clothes Everywhere

All around the world, people wear clothes.

People wear different types
of clothes.

Some clothes are very colorful.

Some clothes make us look stylish.

Why Do People Wear Clothes?

Some clothes keep us warm.

Some clothes help to keep us cool.

Some clothes are good for sports.

Some clothes are good for work.

People wear special clothes
for festivals.

Sometimes special clothes show
that a person is important.

Some clothes are good for
a wedding.

Some clothes are good
for dancing.

Sometimes we wear uniforms.

Sometimes we wear costumes
for fun.

Where Do People Get Their Clothes?

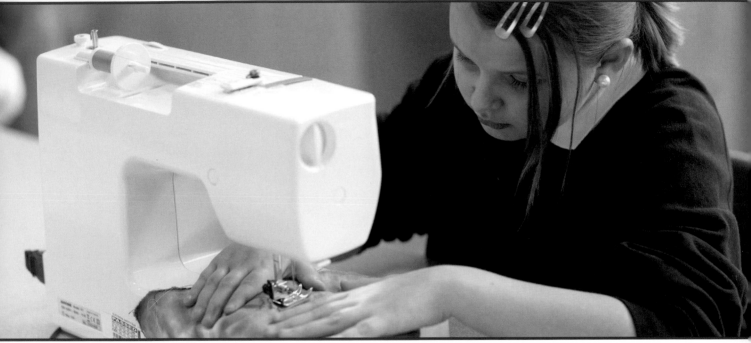

Some people make their own clothes.

Some people buy their clothes.

People wear clothes everywhere.

What do you like to wear?

Map of Clothes Around the World

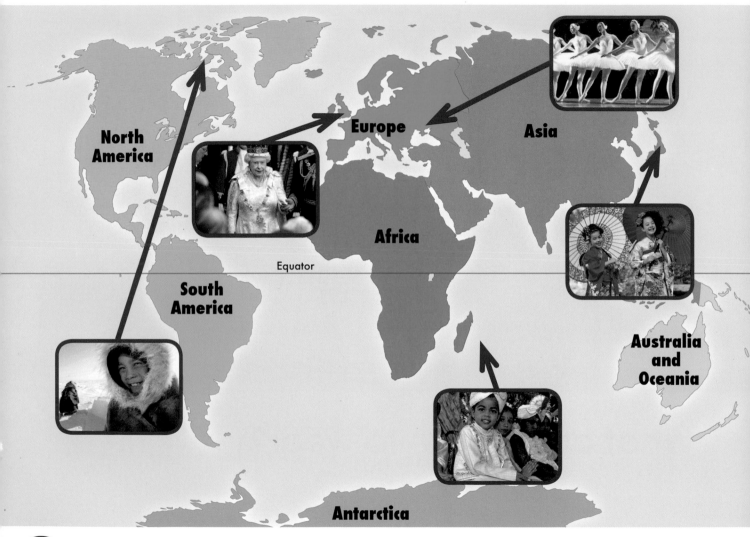

North America

Europe

Asia

Africa

Equator

South America

Australia and Oceania

Antarctica

Picture Glossary

 **costume** type of clothes people wear to look like someone or something else

 **festival** special time for a group of people

 **uniform** clothes that are all the same

Index

Notes for parents and teachers

Before reading

Show children a globe and explain that it is a model of Earth. Discuss how people live all over the world and identify the seven continents, including the continent on which you live. Ask children to think about what they are wearing. When they got dressed, did they think about the weather? Why did they choose to wear what they are wearing? Discuss how people in the community wear many different types of clothes, as do people all over the world.

After reading

- Turn to page 16 and re-read the text. Ask children to define *uniform*. Discuss how the photo illustrates uniforms and have children name other types of uniform.

- Point out the map on page 22. Explain that this map is a flat representation of the globe. Demonstrate for children how to use the map to identify the continents on which different photos from the book were taken.